Monitoring and Investigating Human rights abuses in armed conflict

Amnesty International and CODESRIA

Amnesty International

Council for the Development of Social Science Research in Africa

© Amnesty International and CODESRIA 2001

Amnesty International Dutch Section, Keizersgracht 620, PO Box 1968,1000 BZ Amsterdam, The Netherlands

Council for the Development of Social Science Research in Africa Avenue Cheikh Anta Diop Angle Canal IV, BP 3304 Dakar, Senegal

ISBN 2-86978-110-5

Cover drawing by Lawson B. Sworh

Edited by Chuck Scott

Typesetting by Djibril Fall

Printed in Great Britain by Russell Press Ltd, Basford

Distributed by

Amnesty International Dutch Section, Keizersgracht 620, PO Box, 1968, 1000 BZ Amsterdam, The Netherlands
Fax: 31-020-624-08-89   Email: amnesty@amnesty.nl
web site: www.amnesty.nl

and

African Books Collective, 27 Park End Street, Oxford, OX1, 1HU UK
Fax: 44-01865-793298   Email: abc@dial.pipex.com
web site: www.africanbookscollective.com

Contents

I. Introduction: The role of a human rights defender in armed conflict

Widespread abuses of human rights and international humanitarian law are a common feature of modern conflicts. Civilians, particularly women and children, are the main victims in these wars. Several armed groups terrorise the civilian population to weaken support for their opponents. In some cases government forces attack unarmed civilians because of their ethnic origin or political affiliation. In other situations the state is weak and no longer holds legal authority to protect the weak. In conflicts like these human rights are virtually never respected, despite being protected by international law.

For many years the International Committee of the Red Cross (ICRC) took the leading role in encouraging the application of humanitarian law in situations of international and internal armed conflict. Now an increasing number of human rights organizations are also monitoring respect for humanitarian law in situations of armed conflict. Many development agencies are also considering what their role should be.

Investigating a specific human rights abuse[1] within armed conflict is not so different from investigating the same kind of violation in other situations. However, some features in the process of monitoring and documenting abuses do make a difference and often make it more difficult; for example, the context and working environment, the different parties involved, and the scale of the abuses. There are also new areas to monitor. These include the use of child soldiers and slavery, the importance of human rights considerations in peace agreements and peace-keeping operations, the sale of weapons, and questions about the personal safety and impartiality of the monitor. To examine these issues the editorial advisory committee of UKWELI has decided to publish this booklet in addition to those on monitoring and investigating (i) political killings, (ii) torture, (iii) excessive use of force, (iv) death in custody, and (v) sexual violence.

The booklet starts with a look at monitoring in the context of armed conflict and examines what general information is required to prepare for fact-finding in situations of armed

1
Throughout this text, the term "violation" is used in the same way that Amnesty International and UN use the term. It refers specifically to a clear breach of international human rights law which is formally binding on governments. The term "abuse" is a more general term, which includes reference to the breaking of international humanitarian law by any party in a conflict.

conflict. This is followed by an overview of what sorts of abuses occur in armed conflict and some ideas on how to investigate and verify information relating to each of these specific incidents. The Annexes contain relevant extracts from international and regional human rights law and international humanitarian law. These can be used to clarify the legal basis for investigating, documenting and taking action on abuses.

Armed conflict and humanitarian law[2]

The monitoring and documenting of abuses in armed conflicts is a relatively new area of work for many organizations. This activity requires an understanding of humanitarian law as well as detailed knowledge of the nature of the specific conflict. The four Geneva Conventions of 1949 deal mainly with international armed conflicts, with the exception of article 3, which is common to all four Conventions and deals with 'Conflicts not of an international character'. In 1977 two protocols were adopted which contain rules to protect the civilian population against the effects of hostilities. These are seen as a great step forward in humanitarian law.

Protocol I covers international armed conflicts[3] and extends the application of the 1949 Geneva Conventions to:

armed conflicts in which peoples are fighting against colonial domination and alien occupation and racist regimes in the exercise of their right to self-determination, as enshrined in the Charter of the United Nations...

Protocol II[4] substantially supplements and develops Common article 3 (the only previous provision which covered internal armed conflict) and only applies to internal armed conflicts. These are defined as:

armed conflicts ... which take place in the territory of a (party to the convention) ... between its armed forces and dissident armed forces or other organized armed groups which, under responsible command, exercise such control over a part of its territory as to enable them to carry out sustained and concerted military operations and to implement this Protocol. (Article 1.1)

2
See Annex II for international humanitarian law

3
Protocol I has been ratified by over 150 countries

4
Protocol II has been ratified by 149 states

Protocol II also distinguishes internal armed conflict from other internal conflict situations. It states clearly:

> *This Protocol shall not apply to situations of internal disturbances and tensions, such as riots, isolated and sporadic acts of violence and others acts of a similar nature, as not being armed conflicts. (Article 1.2)*

II. How to monitor in the context of armed conflict

Monitoring is the long-term observation and analysis of human rights situations in a country or region. It consists of the systematic and regular collection of information that may be related to human rights abuses.

Information can be obtained from a variety of sources. These include:

- Local, national or international non-governmental organisations
- Religious groups
- Professionals, such as, doctors, lawyers, journalists, trade unionist, etc.
- Members of government and Parliament
- Members of all political parties
- Members of the security forces, the army, police, etc.
- International organisations, UN Agencies
- Diplomats and Embassy staff

This information, collected over a period of time, should allow you to place the cases under investigation within a political, legal and military context, as well as identify patterns of abuses.

1. Relevant information are especially relevant when monitoring human rights abuses in armed conflict?

A. Contextual information, such as:
- **Historical context** of the conflict. How and when did the conflict arise? Who are the main parties in conflict? What are the root-causes behind the conflict? Has the nature of the conflict changed over time?
- **Economic indicators** and how these have been affected by the conflict. This would include examining the impact of sanctions. Where do the resources to maintain the conflict come from? What are the economic factors behind the conflict – minerals, drugs trade etc?
- **Social indicators,** for example, access to land, education and health care. What impact has the conflict had on these indicators and other social services? Are different age, gender, ethnic or political groups of the population affected differently?

- **Demographic data related to population trends** (size, age, male/female, urban/rural). How is this changing in the current period of conflict? Refugees and internally displaced populations would be of particular concern.

B. National and international political information
would include:
- Alliances between and among armed factions and the ethnic/political sympathies of factions;
- Internal and external influences on the parties to the conflict. These could include internal supporters and foreign governments which might be providing direct military support and weapons, supporting resolutions at international fora, offering financial support or safe havens for refugees or fighters, etc;
- Activities of the war: dates and places of attacks, methods used, number allegedly killed, wounded, displaced etc.

C. The legal and constitutional context would include
national and international law, as well as informal systems of justice. For example:
- Legislation governing the use of force by the police, military and other security bodies;
- Legislation governing the written media and broadcasting, including new legislation which may have been introduced during the conflict;
- The role of military courts, the number and types of cases handled, prosecutions and judgements.
- Laws regulating investigations, such as post-mortem procedures and provisions for immunity from prosecution;
- Special legal provisions which apply at time of war, declared states of emergency, formal withdrawal from international legal obligations (known as derogations);
- Whether certain armed groups have their own systems of justice;
- International humanitarian and human rights laws concerning armed conflict (a selection appears in the Annexe);
- Information about new developments, such as the International Criminal Court and precedents in

extradition procedures (e.g. the case against ex-General Pinochet of Chile at the turn of the century);

- The workings of the International Criminal Tribunal for the former Yugoslavia and the International Criminal Tribunal for Rwanda;
- The deadlines of the government's international reporting obligations to various human rights bodies, such as the Human Rights Committee, to allow for the preparation of submissions;
- Any provisions for amnesty laws and how they have been applied in the past. This might prove useful in peace negotiations when issues around how to address human rights abuses will be raised.

D. A comprehensive knowledge of the organisation of the government security and armed *forces* and of other armed groups involved in the conflict will help you establish which party is responsible for specific human rights abuses in the conflict.

(a) Collect information on the organisation of the *government security forces* and monitor changes:

- Identify the different branches within the security forces, establish their area of authority and their respective chains of command. Who makes the decisions and who gives the orders? Who carries out the orders?
- Establish where responsibility lies for holding the military accountable;
- Collect and study various codes of conduct, regulations and internal guidelines regarding the use of lethal force;
- Find out what type of training is provided and whether any foreign countries are involved in the training;
- Research other forms of foreign military assistance;
- Identify which parts of the security forces are usually involved in violating human rights;
- Find out if there are armed independent organisations (paramilitary groups, militias) who support the government and if they receive military training, transport and equipment from the government;
- Identify what sort of security agreements exists (between countries, with the UN etc).

(b) Collect information on the organisation of *armed opposition groups* and monitor changes:

- Identify whether any organizations or parties are organized on a paramilitary basis;
- Identify the various armed factions or branches, their leadership and chain of command;
- Identify their international, regional or national supporters and the nature of their support;
- Identify their sources of weapons, military training and other expertise;
- Identify other sources of funding e.g. pillaging, taxing the local population, trafficking of drugs, minerals etc;
- Monitor the reactions of their leadership to human rights abuses.
- Identify their relationship with the local population. For example, is there a natural alliance or is it ruled by terror?

(c) Collect information on the methods of operation and means of identification of *government security forces* and *armed opposition groups*:

- Identify the type of arms usually used by specific units within the security forces or armed faction;
- Identify the different uniforms for each unit of the security forces or the 'outfits' of the armed groups;
- Identify the ranking system;
- List the various means of transport each unit or armed group tends to use;
- List any other visible signs of identification, e.g. use of language, specific expressions, signals left behind after an operation etc.;
- Identify their most likely victims.
- Collect details of previous operations; identify common patterns in their methods of operation.

Some additional sources of information that may help with this difficult area are:

- The Internet provides reliable reference material about weapons etc. from military publishers;
- Military advisors or personnel attached to diplomatic

missions in the country;
- Military advisors or personnel attached to UN operations, if any;
- Reports available to the public from countries transferring weapons, munitions, or technical expertise (e.g. US Defence Department reports to Congress and the equivalent materials from France, UK, Portugal etc)
- Humanitarian workers who may work in the conflict zone;
- Deserters or other former fighters.

2. How to record and monitor individual cases and incidents

Even though it may not be possible to investigate all incidents of human rights abuses, it is helpful to monitor all cases that come to your attention through the media, family members, or witnesses etc. This will enable you to develop an understanding of the pattern of incidents.
- To help you with monitoring, it is recommended that you develop a form to record individual cases of alleged human rights abuse that are brought to your attention.
- The form is meant to give you a quick look at a case and to identify possible common points among a number of cases.

Below are examples of certain types of data you will need to record individual cases

General data

- Victim identification information
- Location of the incident
- General circumstances of the incident
- Nature of the incident
- Precise circumstances of the incident
- Alleged perpetrators
- Evidence
- Official responses[5]

5
For more details, see other booklet in this series entitled: *Monitoring and Investigating Political Killings.*

3. How to identify patterns:

Below are some examples of the types of patterns you might look for:

- Patterns in the identity of the victims
- Patterns in the circumstances
- Patterns in the locations of the incidents
- Patterns in the methods used
- Patterns in the identity of alleged perpetrators
- Patterns in responses by government forces or armed groups[6]

6
For more details, see other booklet in this series entitled: *Monitoring and Investigating Political Killings.*

III. How to conduct fact-finding

Fact-finding consists of:
- Investigating a specific incident or allegation of human rights abuse;
- Collecting or finding a set of facts that proves or disproves that the incident occurred and how it occurred; and
- Verifying allegations or rumours.

Four main questions should guide your investigation:

1. What kind of evidence do I need to make sure that the particular abuse has occurred?
2. Is it safe to go to the scene?
3. Who is most likely to give me access to the evidence?
4. How can I be sure that the information is reliable?

The following information will help you organise your fact-finding.

1. List facts and evidence[7]

List everything you know about the specific incident and the conflict zone:

- What human rights and humanitarian law issues are raised by the incident?
- Were there previous incidents of the same violation and other violations in the same area?
- Were there recent military activities in the area concerned, and is it land mined?
- What is the latest security situation in the specific area?

Seek expert advice:

- Get all the necessary information or expert advice, for example, consult with medical personnel, lawyers, military experts and other informed sources.

[7] For more detailed advice, refer to the other booklet in this series entitled: *Monitoring and Investigating Political Killings.*

Prepare your interview format

Identify the evidence you need to show that a human rights abuse has occurred and who is responsible – see the "evidence required" section at the end of each abuse listed in "what constitutes an abuse of human rights in armed conflict" in section V of this booklet.

2. Before going (or not) to the scene

Carry out a thorough risk-assessment

This is particularly important in areas of armed conflict.

If you decide not to go to the scene, it is important to devise an alternative strategy. This will include making use of all other sources of information.

If you decide to go to the scene of some form of human rights abuse, you need to assess all the risks involved for you, your colleagues, and the people you will talk to.

- List all possible security concerns (e.g. your own physical security, and security of your contacts) and develop contingency plans to deal with each of them (e.g. will you be able to leave the area quickly and safely?). If access to the scene and your presence there is too dangerous, identify alternative means of carrying out the research. For example a confidential local contact may be able to bring possible witnesses outside the area.
- A reconnaissance mission would help to find out: the lines of authority in the area, the level of hostilities, the number of check-points you will have to go through, whether or not you need to disguise yourselves, people's reaction and feelings, and whether someone of a different ethnic group or political profile would be safer, etc.
- Be prepared. Have good reasons for your visit and what you are doing in the area in case people ask you difficult questions or appear suspicious.
- If necessary, seek "official" protection in the area. When considering this option, think through the consequences of having an "official" escort – will it jeopardise your impartiality and will people still trust you?

- You should always consider the risks to those you hope to interview. Can you minimise the risks to witnesses who might be prepared to talk to you? Reliable local contacts can help to encourage people to speak to you and may provide the best chance to guarantee their safety after the interview. You should always try not to attract attention to your enquiries and meetings.

Ensure a suitable delegation

Be strategic. Find an experienced delegation, seek out experts, ensure a gender balance and give consideration to ethnicity, language etc.[8] The composition of your delegation will depend on the objective of the mission or field-trip. This may be low- or high-profile (attracting publicity) or have a specific purpose that requires certain expertise, e.g. observing a trial may require a lawyer to be present.

3. Identify and interview relevant sources of information

List all possible contacts and sources of information you may need to interview to investigate and confirm the information.[9] Make a decision about whether you need to meet with security officials and at which point in the investigation.

4. Assess the information

The following is a list of questions and issues that may help you in the investigation:

1. The context:

In a situation of armed conflict, there is likely to be much misinformation promoting one cause or another. When receiving and analysing information, always ask: what does the source of the information stand to gain from this story? It is important to collect and check information from a wide variety of sources.

8
The issue of a suitable delegation is more fully explored in the other booklets in this series. See *UKWELI*, page 11

9
More details about suggested sources of information are provided in the other booklets in this series. See *UKWELI*, page 13

Some situations tend to lead to more abuses. These might be:
- during negotiations between factions;
- in reaction to certain statements by an opposing side;
- a state of despair within an armed faction;
- after criticism at home or before an international audience,
- retaliation for attacks or recent defeats.

2. The victim(s): is there anything that suggests why the victims have been targeted?

- Are the victims "legitimate targets"? Not all killings in armed conflicts are illegal. For instance, armed forces are not prohibited from killing individuals who take a direct part in hostilities, such as soldiers, members of armed opposition groups, etc. People taking part in hostilities may be killed under the laws of war, as long as they are not prisoners or have not put down their arms. Such lawful killings do <u>not</u> constitute an abuse of human rights. (See Articles 43-47 from Optional Protocol I in Annex II.)
- Is there any apparent motive for the killing? Had these individuals or group been previously threatened or targeted? By whom?

3. The circumstances: do they point to involvement of the security forces or of a particular armed group?

- Which soldiers or armed group members were seen at the scene of the incident?
- What were their identifying characteristics? What vehicle? What "uniform"?
- Which group was in control of the area?
- Which groups have been active in the area?

4. The method: does it suggest the involvement of government forces or a particular armed group?

- Has this method of repression been used before by a particular branch of the government security forces or by a particular armed group?

By gathering details about the incident itself, the sequence of events, the way the abuse was carried out and the way the perpetrators left the scene, you will be better able to identify which group may have been responsible.

5. Responses to the incident:

- Was there any public response to the incident? Did any group claim or deny responsibility?
- Has any party agreed to carry out an investigation into the incident?
- Has anyone been held responsible for the incident?

IV. Checking your information—What is sufficient proof?

Human rights organizations should decide the level of proof they want to achieve before they start monitoring. The standard of proof guides the quantity and quality of evidence that has to be gathered in order to support certain conclusions. [10]

In the course of gathering facts, human rights organizations need to determine if they have obtained 'sufficient proof' to arrive at reasonable conclusions. Otherwise, fact-finding can become a never-ending process.

The normal rules of evidence followed by courts require different proof for different levels of liability. For example, in Anglo-Saxon criminal law, the guilt of the accused must be proved "beyond a reasonable doubt" during hearings before an impartial court. The court must hear 'both sides', the evidence against the accused and arguments in their defence. In most cases, human rights organizations are not able to attain this level, partly because they do not have the power to compel witnesses to testify or produce documents, and cannot impose sentences for withholding evidence. However, where possible, human rights organizations should strive to attain the level of "beyond reasonable doubt" in their investigations. Another level of proof is the "balance of probabilities". This is used in civil trials that do not involve the loss of liberty of the defendant.

Level of proof

[10]
This section is reproduced and slightly revised from "Monitoring State-sponsored violence in Africa", ARTICLE 19, January 2000. We would like to thank ARTICLE 19 for making this material available

The level of proof used by human rights organizations depends on the action that is planned for after the fact-finding.

Example: A letter of concern sent to the authorities may only need credible second-hand reports of human rights violations. However, a major report meant for publication would require more substantial evidence on the violations.

If the government normally contests every fact in a human rights report the level of proof needs to be high. You should try and get the government to undertake their own fact-finding and to disclose the results of their investigations.

The level of proof may also depend on the readership of the report.

Example: Some of the UN agencies require a higher level of proof before taking action on allegations of torture.

You may discover pieces of evidence of varying weight and persuasiveness. Consistency and care should be taken when compiling the findings. The final report should state the standard of proof that has been used.

You should show in the report how certain the level of evidence is. In most reports incidents that are not 100 per cent established can be included, as long as the level of probability is disclosed.

Example: If there is not enough evidence to "definitely conclude", the case can still be presented as "very likely", "probable", "eyewitnesses stated that" or in similar phrases.

When reporting on sudden crisis situations there may not be enough time to check all the facts and make a comprehensive report. It is NOT a good idea to use less than a minimum level of proof to make statements concerning the situation. Reports (emergency bulletins) made in such situations should be written in a qualified way so that, if a mistake is made, the organization is not bound by it.

Example: Emergency reports on crisis situations should use qualifying terms such as "witnesses say that" and "we are unable to verify at the moment" to indicate the sources and status of the information.

There should be some consistency in the level of proof used from report to report, unless there is a good reason to change it.

Example: If a particular form of punishment is described as torture in one report, it should not be changed without giving reasons in later reports.

There have been some attempts to categorise levels of proof. *Example*: The United Nations Truth Commission in El Salvador had three levels of proof. First was "overwhelming proof", which meant highly convincing proof. The second was "substantial proof", which was solid proof in support of the conclusion. Finally, "sufficient proof", was proof in support, rather than in contradiction, of the conclusion. The Truth Commission also worked on the basis that no source or witness by itself was sufficient to establish the truth on any vital fact.

Human rights organizations using these rules may be delayed in reaching conclusions in cases where they have some evidence to believe that human rights violations are occurring, but not enough to prove them.

Admissions against interest

Governments often tend to totally deny reports and allegations of human rights violations. However, by publishing credible reports, human rights organizations can succeed in forcing governments to acknowledge the findings of investigations.

Example: A human rights organization may publish a report with numerous cases of disappearances. The government may respond by admitting that only a few cases have occurred.

The organization may accept the government's admission, against its own interest, as a fact or as a minimum figure for the number of confirmed cases of disappeared.

Whenever possible, government officials should be interviewed. Such interviews may provide information and clues that are useful to the investigation. In cases where a government refuses to meet human rights organizations, or remains silent despite the publication of credible reports, its silence cannot automatically be taken as an admission of guilt.

However, the government's refusal to meet with human rights groups can be shown as an indication of a lack of commitment to human rights. The fact that the government was given a chance to present its side can be used to show, at the very least, that the fact-finding was undertaken fairly.

Burden of proof

When a human rights organization reports that human rights violations have taken place, the burden of proof rests on the government to show that this was not the case, or that government agents were not responsible for the violations.

Burden of proof (or onus) is another way of showing whose turn it is to respond to the evidence—the organization engaged in fact-finding or the government. Obviously, human rights organizations always want the onus to be on the government. They must first show sufficient evidence to shift the burden to the government. A primary purpose of human rights investigations is to find the truth, or the nearest thing to it, and present it in such a way as to shift the burden of proof to the government—to make them respond and take some action. At each step, the evidence has to be enough to shift the burden back to the government. What is "enough" varies.

V. What constitutes an abuse of human rights in armed conflict?

When deciding on what is an abuse of human rights, it is important to understand the accepted definitions of armed conflict, civilians and members of the armed forces from the perspective of international humanitarian law. These are covered in Annexe II, dealing with international humanitarian law.

Below, we look at the following:

- Types of killings
- Torture
- Deliberate mutilations
- Deliberate and indiscriminate attacks on the civilian population
- Particular abuses against children
- Rape and other forms of sexual violence
- Use of hate speech to incite violence against others
- Unfair trials in armed conflict – ending impunity and summary justice
- Displacement/refugee populations – the rights of refugees and internally displaced people
- Hostage-taking

After each type of abuse, there is a list of evidence required and possible sources for the information.

As with any other party in armed conflict, peacekeepers are equally bound by international human rights and humanitarian law. Violations by peacekeeping forces should be researched and documented in the same way as those committed by government forces and armed opposition groups.[11]

11
A useful source of information here is the UN Secretary General's Bulletin on Observance by UN Forces of International Humanitarian Law (available on the Internet at www.un.org/peace).

A. Types of killings

Definition, in summary:

1. Not all killings are human rights abuses

- Many are crimes that are handled under criminal law, e.g. when a robber kills a shop owner.

- Some killings by the state do not violate international human rights standards. For example, if a person is killed as a result of police using the minimum force necessary to protect life, the killing is not unlawful.

2. Killings are human rights violations when they are murders directly committed by the authorities or condoned by the authorities. They must show the following three characteristics:

- **They take place at the order, complicity or with the agreement of the authorities.** Killings carried out by individual police officers or soldiers in violation of enforced orders do not constitute human rights violations unless they go unpunished or are ignored by the authorities.
- **They are deliberate:** They have NOT occurred by accident or because of ignorance or self-defence.
- **They are unlawful:** They violate national laws such as those prohibiting murder, as well as international human rights and humanitarian standards forbidding arbitrary deprivation of life. They did not follow proper and adequate judicial or legal proceedings.

3. Killings constitute human rights abuses when they violate the laws of war prohibiting the killing of unarmed individuals and prisoners of war. Such violations include:

- Deliberate killing of prisoners of war
- Deliberate killing of civilians

4. Killings by an armed opposition group constitute human rights abuses when they violate international norms prohibiting the arbitrary deprivation of life. That is:

- They are **deliberate**. They are not committed in self-defence, by accident or ignorance;
- They disobey the minimum standards of human behaviour which apply to both governments and armed opposition groups;
- They are committed **on the authority of a political entity** or with its consent. The killings are part of a policy to eliminate specific individuals or groups or categories, or they occur because they are tolerated and are allowed to be committed.[12]

Examples of armed conflict killings that *are* human rights abuses:

Category 2 above:

"On 3 March 1997, at least 150 unarmed civilians, and possibly as many as 280, were killed by RPA soldiers in a military search operation in the communes of Kigombe, Nyakinama and Mukingo, in Ruhengeri, one day after an attack by an armed group in the town of Ruhengeri in which several people were reportedly killed. The RPA carried out large-scale "cordon and search" operations in several locations in the area; soldiers – reportedly assisted by gendarmes – reportedly rounded up local residents from their homes, led them away and shot them or beat them to death." (Rwanda: Ending the silence. *Amnesty International 25 September 1997)*[13]

Category 3 above:

In August 1998, combatants of the opposition alliance known as the Rassemblement congolaise pour la démocratie (RCD), Congolese Rally for Democracy, together with Rwandese soldiers reportedly killed 37 people, including Stanislas Wabulakombe, a Roman Catholic priest, and three nuns at Kasika Roman Catholic parish and as many as 850

12
Please see booklet in this series entitled: *Monitoring and investigating political killings* for a full exploration of this subject.

13
The authorities recognized the excessive use of force in these incidents and several officers allegedly involved in this operation were reported to have been arrested after these killings.

other unarmed civilians in surrounding villages. (Amnesty International Report 1999, p.139).

Example of armed conflict killings that are *not* human rights abuses:

The laws of war make some killings in armed conflict lawful and therefore not an abuse of human rights. For example, killing as a result of armed combat between different factions or between government troops and an armed faction.

Fact-finding – Establish how the incident fits into the patterns you have already identified. You will then need to collect the following evidence.

Evidence required:

Were the victims civilians?
> => **If yes,** was the killing deliberate and not accidental? Was the killing arbitrary?
> To answer these questions, you will need the following information:
> - Were civilians given a warning to leave the area?
> - Was it clear to the perpetrators that the victims were non-combatants, or were they accidentally caught up in the context of fighting?
> - Was the attack specifically aimed at civilians and was it persistent?

If civilians were warned to leave the area and the answer to the other two questions is no, for example, the civilians were killed by mistake as a result of a skirmish between two armed groups, the killing is NOT an abuse of human rights.

If the victims were combatants.
> => Had the victim already been detained or disarmed by the attacker? It is a violation of humanitarian law to kill anyone who is "detained", including military or security personnel who are no longer taking part in hostilities.

For killings as a result of deliberate and indiscriminate attacks on the civilian population (e.g. by use of shells or landmines), please see Section D below.

Possible sources:
- Military observers
- Eyewitnesses
- Hospital staff
- NGO workers operating in the area.

B. Torture

The following is an extract from the booklet in this series entitled: *Monitoring and Investigating torture, cruel, inhuman or degrading treatment, and prison conditions* which provides full information about the evidence required and possible sources.

II - Armed groups and torture

The definition of torture raises an important question. Acts of torture have to be committed by, or at the instigation of, or with the agreement of state officials. Does this mean that the word "torture" cannot be used with reference to armed groups? The response is "No"—armed groups may also be held accountable for acts of torture, as shown in the examples below:

- In a conflict situation all armed groups are required to abide by the Geneva Convention which governs the laws and customs of war. The laws of war prohibit torture by all parties in a conflict.[14]

- Armed groups are always responsible for any acts of torture committed by their forces.

- As a human rights worker investigating torture by armed groups, you will not be in a position to refer to the international convention on torture because the perpetrators are members of an armed group. However you can refer to the laws of war and state that all parties to a conflict are prohibited from perpetrating acts of torture and acts of indecent assault (which includes

14
Non-Governmental Organisations such as Amnesty International apply the definition of torture to acts committed by members of armed groups.

rape and other forms of sexual assault against women, men or children).

Examples

The following are the testimonies of children and adults caught up in the conflict between the Ugandan government and an armed opposition group, the Lord's Resistance Army (LRA).

A 17-year-old girl, abducted by the LRA, described what happened to her when she tried to escape:

"I was seen by the rebels staying up in the trees. They caught me and punished me for trying to escape. "The teacher tortured me. He poured boiling oil on my hand."

A woman describes what happened to her family during an LRA attack on her village:

"I was sitting in my home with my six-month-old baby. The rebels arrived. They picked the baby from me and threw him on the ground. He survived. My husband was a civil servant. He was there, along with a man who had come to buy groundnuts. The rebels started beating them. They killed my husband. They did not kill the buyer but he is now mentally deranged. Then they started raping me. My daughter was seven years old. They burnt her with fire, tortured her and asked her where my husband had put government property. I was also beaten on the head and lost my teeth."

The case of Ibrahima Mané

Ibrahima Mané, a 19-year-old pupil at the Koranic school in Kaolack, left Niaguis in mid-March 1998 for Ziguinchor to obtain his identity papers. At Adéane he was arrested by soldiers who tortured and ill-treated him. His body was burned using pots of melted plastic and burning ash was spread over him. He was then transferred to Zinguinchor where he was detained for 37 days at the command post of the southern military zone. He escaped on the night of Friday 24 April and was able to contact RADDHO which raised the case with the Senegalese Committee for Human Rights and arranged for a lawyer to defend him. He is still waiting as no inquiry into his case has been opened to this day.

From RADDHO's annual report 1998-1999.

C. Deliberate mutilations

Additional Protocol II of the Geneva Conventions, Article 4, specifically outlaws this particular form of torture. See Annex II.

Example: In April 1998 in Sierra Leone, rebel forces embarked on a campaign of terror against civilians which they called "Operation no living thing". The following figures are from a report by Medicins Sans Frontières in May 1998:

As of 6th April 1998 Connaught Hospital started receiving small or large groups, depending on the availability of transport. By early May 1998 some 115 victims of severe mutilation had been admitted to this hospital in the centre of Freetown; about 60 were admitted on one day alone, 26 April 1998. The report gives the following overview of the wounds:

- 4 men with both arms amputated, age ranging between 16 and 40.
- 14 men with one arm amputated, age ranging between 23 and 50.
- 5 men had, in addition to having their arm(s) amputated, a part of, or one or both ears cut off.
- 1 woman with one arm amputated as a result of a gunshot wound.
- 1 patient with an amputated foot, 1 patient with an amputated leg, both as result of gunshot wounds.
- 23 patients with deep lacerations on lower arms, severed tendons, broken ulna and radius, as result of cutlass attacks.
- 7 patients with either a complete hand or several fingers

missing as result of cutlass attacks.
- 20 patients with gunshot wounds.
- 1 patient with shrapnel wounds as result of ECOMOG*
bombing.
- 2 women who were raped and had foreign objects inserted in their vagina.

Only one of these victims could be identified as a combatant (in this case a Kamajor fighter). All others were civilians, with occupations ranging from housewives, trader, farmer to diamond digger and miner. (*Atrocities against civilians in Sierra Leone* – Médicins Sans Frontières, May 1998.)

*
ECOWAS Monitoring
Group

D. Deliberate or indiscriminate attacks on the civilian population

Definition

Deliberate or indiscriminate killing of civilians in armed conflict are unlawful killings of civilians during an attack by an armed force under the control of a government or opposition group. The armed force either intentionally or recklessly disregards its obligation to direct attacks only at military objectives and to distinguish between military and civilian targets.

The definition of deliberate or indiscriminate killings of civilians includes several elements:

- Such killings are **unlawful** because they are an arbitrary deprivation of the right to life and violate fundamental rules of the laws of war.
- Such killings are carried out by **armed forces under the control of a government or an armed opposition group.**
- Such killings take place during **attacks occurring in the course of an armed conflict.**[15]
- Such killings are the result of an armed force **either intentionally (deliberate) or recklessly (indiscriminate) disregarding its obligation to distinguish** between military objectives and civilians or civilian objects.
- Those killed are **civilians, or non-combatants.**

15
The rules governing the conduct of hostilities are different depending on the nature of the armed conflict. It could be an international armed conflict (involving armed forces operating outside their own territory) or an internal armed conflict. Direct attacks against civilians are prohibited in both types of conflict, but prohibitions on indiscriminate attacks are only *explicitly* set out in the rules governing international armed conflicts (including certain wars of "national liberation"), which also include more rules regarding the protection of civilians against the effects of hostilities.
(...)

The following are some *examples* of an *indiscriminate attack:*

- Attacks which are not directed at a specific military objective, e.g. "blind fire" and orders for aircrews to release bombs anywhere over enemy territory before returning to base;
- Attacks which treat a number of clearly distinct and separated military objectives as one military objective, e.g. "area bombardment";
- Attacks that cannot be directed against a specific military target, usually because the weapons are not able to make a distinction between civilian and military targets (e.g. long-range missiles with questionable accuracy).
- Disproportionate attacks,[16] for example, one aimed at a legitimate military target but which has a disproportionate impact on civilians.

Example of Disproportionate attacks:

Between April and June 1999, the Mouvement des forces démocratiques de Casamance (MFDC), Democratic Forces of Casamance Movement, fired several shells in and around Ziguinchor, the capital of the Casamance region of southern Senegal, including at the airport. It appears the later shells were a response to a raid by the Senegalese army, designed to dislodge MFDC fighters. All the victims of the shellings were civilians, attacked in their homes or in the street. (See: *Senegal – Casamance civilians shelled by the MFDC,* Amnesty International, 30 June 1999, for more details.)

Such use of force violates Common Article 3 of the four Geneva Conventions of 1949 and the second protocol of the Geneva Convention of 1977, in particular Article 13.

Fact-finding – Evidence required:

When alleged unlawful killings of civilians are the result of an attack by artillery, mortar or other "crew-served weapons" (tanks, mobile artillery, rocket launchers, etc.) the following factors should be considered:

- What, if any, legitimate military objectives were in the area attacked?
- How important were the military objectives?

(contd.)
However, some NGOs, such as Amnesty International, equally oppose indiscriminate attacks in internal conflict. The rules on the conduct of hostilities in Protocol I are aimed at protecting civilians and include the principle of distinction, the prohibition of direct and indiscriminate attack, and a list of necessary precautions (see Annexe II). These are accepted as customary for international armed conflict and are binding on countries that are not party to Protocol I.

16
Customary law for international conflict prohibits disproportionate attacks (see Protocol I, 51(5)(b)).

- What were the rules of engagement?
- What type of weapons system was used and what was its accuracy? Take into account the range at which it was fired, the size of the military target, the weather and other conditions (including any immediate threats to those firing it) affecting its accuracy.
- What type and quantity of ammunition was used in the attack?
- How many civilians were killed or injured? How many military personnel were killed or injured?
- What was the scale of damage to civilian objects and to military objectives?
- What degree of knowledge or intelligence did the attacking force have of the areas under attack?
- What, if any, type of system was used by the attacking force to locate the target they were aiming at (forward observers, aerial surveillance, radar systems)?
- Were they firing from fixed or mobile emplacements? (Generally, weapons are more accurate when fired from fixed emplacements.)
- What was the timing and duration of the attack?
- Was the attack pre-planned, or was it an attack on a "target of opportunity"?

When alleged unlawful killings of civilians are the result of an attack from the air, the following additional factors should be considered:

- What type of aircraft was used in the attack?
- What type of munitions were used? Were they precision-guided munitions?
- Did those firing from the aircraft have visual contact with the target?
- From what height and distance from the target did the attack take place?
- What were the rules of engagement?
- What sort of intelligence did the attackers have?
- What was the military objective?
- Were they attacking a fixed target?

Possible sources of information:

- Eyewitnesses to the attack itself or to preparations for the attack, including the military force involved
- People who visited the site of the attack shortly afterwards (could include journalists, diplomatic staff, medical relief workers)
- Medical staff who treated casualties
- Military personnel
- Civilian authorities, including local national Red Cross or Red Crescent.
- Military advisors or personnel attached to any UN operations
- Military advisors or personnel attached to diplomatic missions
- Field staff of the International Committee of the Red Cross.

E. Particular abuses against children:

(a) The detention of children:

Children detained by the security forces or by armed opposition groups may be particularly at risk if held in unofficial places of detention. It is important to trace their place of detention and ensure that they are allowed visits by the International Committee of the Red Cross, their family, medical personnel, lawyers and NGOs working in the field of human rights or human welfare.

(b) The use of child soldiers:

In addition to protection of basic human rights, children are also protected specifically by the UN Convention on the Rights of the Child and by the Additional Protocol II of 8 June 1977 relating to the Protection of Victims of Non-International Armed Conflicts. These two legal texts lay down a minimum age of fifteen years for soldiers.

However, a draft optional protocol to the Convention on the Rights of the Child sets 18 years as the minimum age for participation in hostilities.[17] The draft optional protocol would also prohibit the compulsory recruitment by Governments of persons below 18 years and ban recruitment or use in hostilities of persons under 18 by other armed groups. The document raises the standards contained in article 38 of the Convention on the Rights of the Child and shows a willingness to take stronger measures to keep children out of armed conflicts.

(c) Children as sexual slaves:

In some circumstances, the abduction and forced ownership of children by an army or armed group can be consistent with the international definition of slavery.[18]

Example of abduction and slavery:

Discipline within the Lord's Resistance Army (LRA) is maintained by extreme and arbitrary violence. LRA commanders force captured children to take part in the almost ritualized killing of others very soon after their abduction. The intention appears to be to break down resistance to LRA authority, to destroy taboos about killing and to implicate the child in criminal acts. The effect is to terrorize children... There is no discrimination on gender grounds when it comes to making abducted children kill those who try to escape...Each abducted child is allocated to a "family" headed by a commander... The powers of the men at the head of each family, under the overall authority of Joseph Kony (LRA leader) and other senior commanders, are such that they effectively "own" the children allocated to them as chattels. Girls are held in forced marriages. Commanders have the power to impose hard labour and physical punishment – and the power to kill. In Amnesty International's opinion the degree of ownership over child members of the "family" is such that their condition is consistent with the international definition of slavery. (*UGANDA–"Breaking God's commands": The destruction of childhood by the Lord's Resistance Army*, Amnesty International, 18 September 1997.)

17
A working group of the United Nations Commission on Human Rights, 21 January 2000

18
Article 1 of the 1926 Slavery Convention defines slavery as: "the status or condition of a person over whom any of the powers of ownership are exercised".

Fact-finding – Monitoring these issues with a view to establishing clear patterns is very important. Once you are aware of the patterns of an armed group or government armed forces, you can start to collect facts about individual cases.

Evidence required:

Child detainees
  • Are children being held?
  • If so, by whom, where and why?

Child soldiers
  • Are children under the age of fifteen involved in combat?
  • Which armed groups does this apply to?
  • What are the names of the child soldiers?
  • What are the details of their activities?
  • Can you confirm their account of activities with evidence from other sources about the operations of that group and the weapons mentioned?
  • Can you obtain a statement from a spokesperson from an armed group about the use of child soldiers?
  • Is there psychological evidence that a child has been involved in combat?

Children as sexual slaves
  • Trace events since the child's abduction;
  • Identify the power relations between the armed group and the captives;
  • What activities was the child involved in?
  • Was there a difference between the activities expected of children of different ages and gender?
  • Did the child have an opportunity to refuse certain activities?
  • Is there medical evidence that a child has been sexually abused?
  • Is there psychological evidence that a child has been sexually abused

Sources:
  • The children themselves. It may be difficult to interview

young children and traumatised children. It is unlikely that you will gather all the information you need in one session with a child. Be aware that the child's perception of their experience may be quite different from yours – try to see their story through their eyes;

- Drawings made by the children;
- Their parents/guardians/counsellors or others the children are able to trust;
- Medical records (these may be useful to provide evidence that a child has been sexually abused);
- Security forces or others responsible for detaining them;
- Eyewitnesses.

F. Rape and other forms of sexual violence

Rape by agents of a state or other officials is classified as torture in the Convention against Torture and Other Cruel, Inhuman or Degrading Treatment or Punishment. Rape causes "severe pain or suffering, whether physical or mental", it is intentional, and it has the purpose of punishing, intimidating or coercing.[19]

Example: Mariatu, now aged 16 years, was abducted from the village of Mamamah, some 40 kilometres from Freetown, as rebel forces retreated from the capital in January 1999. Both her parents were killed by rebel forces when they attacked the village. Mariatu was repeatedly gang-raped by a number of rebels. If she attempted to resist rape she was denied food and beaten. She was forced to accompany rebel forces first to Lunsar and then to Makeni and was eventually forced to become the "wife" of one of the rebels. Many other girls were held in the same situation. When she became pregnant, she was taken back to her family and abandoned. (*Sierra Leone, Rape and other forms of sexual violence against girls and women,* Amnesty International, 29 June 2000)

(a) Rape as a war crime:

- Rape is also classified as a war crime because it is a violation of the laws of war, which is "committed by persons 'belonging' to one party to the conflict against persons ... of the other side."[20]

19
See other booklets in this series entitled: *Monitoring and Investigating Sexual Violence* and *Monitoring and InvestigatingTorture, Cruel, Inhuman or Degrading Treatment, and Prison Conditions*

- More specifically, the Fourth Geneva Convention (Article 27, paragraph 2), which applies to areas considered occupied territory, states:

  "Women shall be especially protected against any attack on their honour, in particular against rape, enforced prostitution or any form of indecent assault."

- Article 4 of the Second Protocol of the Geneva Convention which regulates internal armed conflicts expressly forbids: "outrages upon personal dignity, in particular humiliating and degrading treatment, rape, enforced prostitution and any form of indecent assault."

- The International Criminal Court (ICC) Statute gives the ICC the power to try cases of rape or other sexual abuse as war crimes and, when committed on a widespread or systematic basis, as crimes against humanity.

(b) Rape as a crime against humanity:

The Statutes of the International Tribunal for Yugoslavia and the International Tribunal for Rwanda list rape as a crime against humanity. To prove rape as a crime against humanity, the following must be established:

- it must be directed against civilian populations;
- it must be widespread or large-scale, i.e. the rapes must be directed against a number of victims. Single or isolated acts fall outside the scope;
- it must be part of a systematic pattern of abuse through a pre-conceived plan or policy, of which rape is an element. In these circumstances, rape has become a weapon of war;
- it must be committed by state actors (e.g. soldiers, police etc) or by non-state actors (e.g. members of armed opposition groups, individuals acting at the direction of state officials or members of political groups, or with their consent or knowledge). This excludes inhuman acts

20
Meron, 1993, quoted in paper on 'The International Legal Status of Rape', Agnès Callamard, February 1997.

committed by individuals on their own initiative or as part of criminal actions.

(c) Rape as genocide:

Under international humanitarian law, rape can be categorised as genocide. The Convention on the Prevention and Punishment of the Crime of Genocide defines genocide to mean:

"Any of the following acts committed with the intent to destroy, in whole or in part, a national, ethnic, racial or religious group as such ... (b) causing serious bodily harm to members of the group; (c) deliberately inflicting on the group conditions of life calculated to bring about its physical destruction in whole or in part; (d) imposing measures intended to prevent births within the group."

Under international law genocide is a crime in times of peace and armed conflict, whether international or internal.

For details about evidence required and possible sources please see booklet entitled: *Monitoring and Investigating Sexual Violence.*

G. Use of hate speech to incite violence against others

"Hate speech" and other types of expression, which advocate war, and religious or racial hatred is a specific limitation to the right to freedom of expression. Article 19 of the International Covenant on Civil and Political Rights defends freedom of expression, while Article 20 stipulates:

1. Any propaganda for war shall be prohibited by law.
2. Any advocacy of national, racial or religious hatred that constitutes incitement to discrimination, hostility or violence shall be prohibited by law.

It is important to note that the phrase "that constitutes incitement" requires that the views must not only be advocacy of unacceptable and dangerous views, but advocacy which may incite others to action. The freedom of expression community has often argued that the best antidote to hate speech is more speech – thereby extending pluralism rather than restricting it. Hate speech has previously been used mainly by small extremist groups. However, in Rwanda hate speech was used as an important tool for the widespread organisation of genocide. Since then, it has been used in the same way in Burundi and the Democratic Republic of Congo.

Evidence required:

- To establish the context,
  => what are the restrictions on other types of media?
  => has there been a change in the treatment of the independent media?
  => who owns and/or controls the various media outlets?
  => what are their political/ethnic/religious affiliations?

- What is the nature of broadcasts or written material that may represent advocacy of "hatred that constitutes incitement to ..."? Keep copies of written material, transcribe radio or TV broadcasts.
- Can you reveal a correlation between the material and violence? Take care to avoid simple deductions – these have often been used to introduce censorship and destroy freedom of expression, for example where film and TV violence has been inconclusively blamed for leading directly to an increase in violent crimes.
- Can you prove "direct and public incitement to commit genocide" or an "attempt to commit genocide" or "complicity in genocide"? All of these are outlawed by the Convention on the Prevention and Punishment of the Crime of Genocide.
- Can you obtain evidence of the State's failure to "stop incitement to violence"? Both the International Convention on the Elimination of All Forms of Racial Discrimination and the International Covenant on Civil and Political Rights require governments to take concrete measures against violence and incitement to violence based on ethnic hatred.

Possible sources:

- TV/Radio personnel
- Journalists
- Foreign radio stations which may monitor national or local broadcasts
- Freedom of expression NGOs inside or outside the country

H. Unfair trials in armed conflict – ending impunity and summary justice

International humanitarian law contains important safeguards for fair trials. These apply to various categories of people during international wars and internal conflict, including civil wars.[21]

When armed groups establish their own forms of justice:

Armed factions may administer their own form of justice – for example, between 1990 and 1992, Charles Taylor effectively organised his territory as "Greater Liberia" and led a government with a full range of ministers, including one responsible for justice.

Trials that take place in such circumstances are regulated by the 1977 Additional Protocol to the Geneva Conventions of 12 August 1949, and Relating to the Protection of Victims of Non-International Armed Conflicts (Protocol II), Article 6. See Annexe II.

Evidence required:

Was the person found guilty by a court offering the essential guarantees of independence and impartiality? In particular;

- Was the accused informed of the alleged offence and allowed a defence before and during the trial?
- Was the person tried on the basis of individual responsibility?
- Was the person innocent until proven guilty?
- Was the accused present at the trial?
- Did the accused have legal representation at the trial?

21
Please refer to Chapter 32 of the Fair Trials Manual, Amnesty International 1998 (available on http://www.amnesty.org)

If the answer to any of these questions is no,
OR, if the accused was compelled to testify against himself or to confess guilt,
OR, if death penalties were passed against persons under the age of eighteen years at the time of the offence or carried out on pregnant women or mothers of young children, then the trial contravenes the provisions of the Geneva Convention, Protocol II, Article 6.

When the judicial system remains operational:

When a conflict is only affecting part of a country, it is possible that the judicial system will continue to operate.

Uganda is a good example:

The war in northern Uganda pitches the government's Uganda Peoples' Defence Forces (UPDF) against the Lord's Resistance Army (LRA), yet the main victims are civilians. The UPDF has reacted to pressure from NGOs and stopped the army from punishing their own staff for criminal acts. Instead, the police force plays a role in holding the military accountable for their actions by taking responsibility for detaining those handed over by the military, bringing criminal charges and organising trials in civilian courts. However, policing and criminal investigation remains a challenge in the circumstances of armed conflict. For example:

- Politically motivated allegations and counter-allegations are rife;
- The obstacles to locating and protecting witnesses are immense;
- The police are lightly armed and are a target of the LRA. They need the protection of the UPDF if they are to function outside of the main towns;
- Courts have difficulties functioning; and
- It seems the political will to punish the army is absent – between January 1996 and April 1998, the police charged 82 soldiers with serious crimes against the person, but in only three cases, involving 8 soldiers, have there been trials and convictions. (*Uganda – Breaking the circle: Protecting human rights in the northern war zone*, Amnesty International 17 March 1999)

Evidence required:

- You will need a comprehensive knowledge of how the criminal investigation and prosecution service works in normal circumstances to establish the particular irregularities in the context of armed conflict. This will help you to evaluate whether any irregularities are specifically tolerated to allow the armed forces or a militia close to the authorities to act with impunity. While any shortcoming would constitute an abuse of human rights, it is important to be able to present the information in its context.
- Issues around fairness of trials (as above). Article 14 of the International Covenant on Civil and Political Rights would also apply if an emergency has not been declared and if the country concerned has ratified the Covenant;
- How many soldiers have been charged with serious offences and never brought to trial? What has happened to them? Are they on active duty?
- What happens to soldiers who are released for lack of evidence?
- Are there cases where you have good information to report a suspected crime?

When there is no administration of justice:

In many armed conflicts, the administration of justice is an early casualty and it is not until a peace agreement has been signed that the question of impunity can be addressed. In these circumstances, the facts and evidence you are collecting may prove vital to holding perpetrators accountable at the end of the conflict.

Evidence required:

The evidence required is as listed above under the other categories. It should be compiled and kept in a way that is presentable to relevant legal structures. This could include a war crimes tribunal, a commission for truth, justice and reconciliation, etc.

Possible sources:

- Lawyers
- Judges
- Court clerks
- Journalists
- Defendants themselves

I. Displacement/refugee populations – the rights of refugees and internally displaced people[22]

International humanitarian law allows for the displacement of civilians in certain circumstances, for example, for their security or for military reasons. All possible measures must be taken to ensure the shelter, hygiene, health, safety and nutrition of the civilian population.[23] However, civilian populations can be at increased risk if they are displaced.

Example: In northern Uganda, the government created camps for displaced people in reaction to the scale of LRA violence against villagers. However, the authorities failed to guarantee food security and provide adequate protection from violence in camps (or for communities in areas where camps have not been created). Lack of food has meant that in some areas villagers have returned home to cultivate or forage for food, which has exposed them to human rights abuse. The authorities have failed to demonstrate, in Gulu District at least, steps to minimize displacement. They have not taken effective steps to bring to an end the situation that has caused displacement in the first place. This all raises serious questions about whether continuing action to compel people to leave the countryside remains consistent with international law. (From *Uganda – Breaking the circle,* Amnesty International, 17 March 1999).

22
The internally displaced are in a similar situation to refugees, except that they have not fled across an international border – they remain displaced within their own country.

23
See Article 17 of the Geneva Conventions Additional Protocol II.

Evidence required:

You will need to answer the question:

- If the government or an armed opposition group is displacing the civilian population, are there reasonable measures to ensure their protection and well-being?

For this you will need to know:

- Was the civilian population displaced?
- Is this part of a policy by the government forces or the armed group? How long has this policy existed? What is the declared intention?
- What arrangements are made for the displaced in the new area?
- How are they being treated by the local population?
- What provisions are made for their safety, nutrition, shelter and health?
- Are different groups (for example: on the basis of age, gender, ethnicity, nationality) treated differently?
- Are measures in place to protect the most vulnerable (e.g. women, children, people of a particular ethnic group) and to ensure they are integrated into all programmes?
- Do you have sufficient information to conclude that the group responsible is not taking "all reasonable measures"?

International standards for refugees:

All countries are bound under international refugee law[24] to allow all asylum seekers to enter their territory, to provide adequate protection and to respect the principle of *non-refoulement*.

In addition, Conclusion No.22 of the Executive Committee of the United Nations High Commissioner for Refugees (UNHCR) establishes an international principle that:

- In situations of large-scale influx, asylum-seekers should be admitted to the state in which they first seek refuge.
- If the state is unable to admit them on a durable basis, it should admit them on at least a temporary basis.

24
The UN Convention relating to the Status of Refugees and the OAU Convention governing the specific aspects of refugee problems in Africa

- They should be admitted without any discrimination as to race, political opinion, nationality, country of origin or physical incapacity".

Example: The Guinean authorities became increasingly concerned about the large influx of people from Sierra Leone. On 8 June 1997 120 people from West African countries, about half of them from Sierra Leone, had to remain on board the vessel which brought them as they were refused permission to disembark. The Guinean authorities threatened to deny entry to more boats from Freetown (the Sierra Leonean capital) carrying refugees for reasons of internal security. ...In mid-June 1997 some 3,000 Sierra Leonean refugees trying to cross the border into Guinea at Guékédou were refused entry by the Guinean authorities. (*Sierra Leone: A disastrous set-back for human rights*, Amnesty International, 20 October 1997.)

Evidence required:

Gather information about the international relations between the countries concerned and their previous record on hosting asylum seekers. In addition, you will need to know:
- Identities and/or numbers of those seeking asylum
- What type of people are they – men/women/children, old/young, a particular ethnic group etc.?
- Dates of their arrival, *refoulement,* and return
- Which immigration officials made the decision to not allow the asylum seekers to enter?
- What has happened to the people since their return? If they have been victims of human rights abuse since their return, this will add weight to your case on their behalf.

Interviewing refugees or displaced people

This can be particularly difficult. Remember that they are in a stressful situation away from their families and other familiar situations. They might well have high expectations of what you can offer them – take time to explain your role and your limitations.

Possible sources:

- International refugee bodies, such as the UN High Commission for Refugees (UNHCR) and local/national ones.
- Development agencies which may be providing supplies to refugee groups.
- Port/airport/border staff.

J. Hostage-taking

The United Nations' International Convention Against the Taking of Hostages, which came into force in June 1983, sets out its terms of reference by defining a hostage as:

Article 1:
Any person who seizes or detains and threatens to kill, to injure or to continue to detain another person (hereinafter referred to as the "hostage") in order to compel a third party, namely, a State, an international intergovernmental organization, a natural or juridical person, or a group of persons, to do or abstain from doing any act as an explicit or implicit condition for the release of the hostage commits the offence of taking of hostages ("hostage-taking" within the meaning of the Convention).

Hostage taking is also regulated by humanitarian law (see Article 34 of the Fourth Geneva Convention, Annexe II).

Example: Armed Forces Revolutionary Council (AFRC) forces captured more than 30 UN military and civilian personnel who had gone to the Occra Hills in August with an ECOMOG escort to supervise the release of abducted civilians. Their captors claimed that Johnny Paul Koroma (AFRC leader) was held under duress by RUF forces and that the peace agreement disadvantaged AFRC forces. All were released after six days.

In December Revolutionary United Front (RUF) forces captured two foreign nationals working for Médicins Sans

Frontière (MSF-France), in Kailahun District, Eastern Province, and held them hostage for 10 days in protest against disarmament and demobilization being supervised by UN peace-keeping forces and ECOMOG troops. (*Amnesty International Report 2000*, entry on Sierra Leone, p. 209)

Fact-finding—Evidence required:

- Names and other means of identity of those held;
- Place and date and other circumstances of their abduction;
- Details of statements made by their captors and by those who are expected to fulfil the conditions set by the hostage-takers.

Possible sources:

- NGOs based in the area;
- Families of those abducted;
- Eyewitnesses;
- Those responsible for the hostage taking (be politically aware – getting involved in negotiations yourself could damage your work as a human rights monitor).

VI. Taking action

Taking action in a context of armed conflict is particularly difficult. For example, seeking legal remedies may be impossible while the conflict lasts. Medical remedies and outside publicity become all the more important. To cope with these difficulties, building coalitions is necessary. This could include development NGOs that have access to areas of conflict and are open to collaboration with human rights activists. It could also include working with organisations that offer assistance to ex-child soldiers, play a role in peace negotiations, as well as NGOs working on civil and political rights. There are other additional issues to bear in mind.[25]

Other targets:

1. Third parties who support a particular faction:
You may broaden your activities to include putting pressure on other governments and bodies that are supporting the different parties in the conflict. This requires careful fact-finding to prove the links and to clearly establish for example, that country X is providing faction/country Y with landmines or shells that are being used to indiscriminately attack civilian populations. If evidence is lacking, it may be possible to liaise with human rights groups in the other country to see if they can provide information to help in your assessment of the situation.

2. Actors in the peace process:
Providing participants in the peace process with information about human rights abuses is an important role for human rights activists. This can help to ensure that the issues are addressed as part of any agreements.

[25] This area has also been explored in other booklets in this series and they may provide other useful ideas.

3. International bodies:
UN bodies for example UN Observer Mission in Sierra Leone (UNOMSIL) and UN Human Rights Field Operation for Rwanda (UNHRFOR).

4. UN Treaty bodies which oversee governments' adherence to international standards:

For example, the Committee on the Elimination of Racial Discrimination or the Human Rights Committee (which examines adherence to the International Covenant on Civil and Political Rights).

5. Corporations who have invested in the area of conflict:

They may be able to use their influence to improve respect for human rights or may employ security firms that are themselves responsible for human rights abuses.

6. Companies manufacturing weapons that are used to commit human rights abuses:

They could be informed about the evidence you have gathered and lobbied to ensure they do not provide further weapons that might escalate the level of abuse.

VII. Particular challenges and some solutions

You may face numerous obstacles and problems while monitoring human rights abuses in armed conflicts. This section identifies some of these problems and offers some solutions.

Challenges and possible solutions[26] are:

- Labelling
- Feeling exhausted or depressed
- Logistical problems
- Lack of access to information
- Risks to personal security
- Dealing with traumatised people
- Interviewing suspected perpetrators.

Many of these problems are further complicated by the context of armed conflict. **For example:**

- **Labelling** becomes an even greater problem as the society polarises during the conflict and as each party in the conflict attempts to avoid responsibility for abusing human rights. You might be under pressure to takes sides in the conflict or accused of supporting one of the sides. Negative labelling or intimidation may be aimed at damaging your reputation and credibility. Women are particularly vulnerable to negative labelling from the government, family, friends and colleagues.

  Remedies might include emphasising the accuracy of your information. Ensure that the people you interview understand that your role is not to resolve the conflict, but to create an environment that will help others in this task. Explain your impartial approach. It might also be useful to expand any human rights education programmes to inform the population about humanitarian law and the role of human rights monitors in armed conflict. Issue public responses to any attacks on the reputation of your organisation or its members.

26
For more detailed information see *UKWELI – Monitoring and Documenting Human Rights Violations in Africa* Part 3.

- **Feeling exhausted or depressed** is a great risk with the added stress of an armed conflict situation. You may have witnessed, or experienced, human rights violations. This is likely to have a negative effect on your mental well-being.

This makes the **remedies** suggested all the more important. Insist that your organisation acknowledge the stresses and provide ways of dealing with them. Organise regular debriefing sessions which allow you to talk about your experiences and feelings. Make time to exercise, relax and take part in activities that relieve stress. If the depression or stress is severe, get professional help!

- **Logistical problems** become even greater as all means of communications and existing infrastructure are affected by the conflict. However you have to be adequately prepared and make sure that you have all the necessary equipment and suitable transport if you are in a dangerous situation. Try and get support from other reliable international organisations that are working in the area.

- **Lack of access to information.** During armed conflict people are afraid to speak and there is an even greater lack of public awareness about human rights abuse.

Additional considerations might be whether you can travel to an area without an official escort. If you travel with a government official or an armed opposition group, this could damage your claim to impartiality and the credibility of your work.

However, it is necessary to develop co-operative relations with government and other authorities in order to collect information. Human rights education may also help to encourage people to identify incidents as human rights issues.

- **Risks to personal security** are heightened during travel into areas where hostilities are a possibility and where the parties to the conflict do not wish to see their crimes exposed. Others at risk include your contacts and their family and friends.

=> Precautions include:
  - informing someone of your whereabouts at all times

and particularly if you are travelling to a dangerous zone;
- double-checking any contacts or guides you consider using (are they impartial, seen as impartial, sufficiently knowledgeable about hostilities/safe zones etc?);
- deciding whether to identify yourself as a human rights monitor when going into difficult areas;
- planning what to do in a given zone if you meet problems (such as arrest, abduction etc).
- Is it appropriate to accept an "official" escort?

- **Dealing with traumatised people**: Be aware of how the trauma may affect the person you are interviewing—they may deny the events, exaggerate them or be totally confused. Try to arrange a follow-up meeting with the person you have interviewed to determine the impact of your interview on their psychological state. Also be aware of the impact it may have on you. It will help to talk through the interview with your colleagues, while still respecting confidentiality[27]

- **Interviewing suspected perpetrators**: This is always a difficult situation, made more complex by the heightened tension of the armed conflict. It is important to try to obtain the official story, even though you will need independent sources to verify what you hear and learn. Once you have completed your research, it might also be useful to seek clarification of your allegations with the perpetrators.

It is important to remain polite, even if the spokesperson's version sounds completely incredible. Seek clarification without being confrontational and be prepared to change your view of the situation.

These difficult interviews are best planned in advance. This will allow you to prepare questions you need and give you space to listen to the answers.

[27]
This area is covered in more detail in the first booklet in this series.

Some additional challenges:

Securing a role for human rights monitoring in situations of armed conflict: To protect future human rights it is essential that the international community publicly condemns human rights violations during the conflict, the peace process and once peace is agreed. In a statement to the UN Security Council in September 1999, Mary Robinson, High Commissioner for Human Rights stated:

> *To grant amnesty to the authors of the most atrocious crimes for the sake of peace and reconciliation may be tempting, but it contradicts the purpose and principles of the UN Charter as well as international observed principles and standards.*

National and international human rights organizations play a vital role in providing the information that can help to hold perpetrators accountable. In addition, it is important that international field personnel, including those engaged in military, civilian and humanitarian operations, should not be "silent witnesses". Instead, they should report, through proper channels, any human rights violations they may witness or serious allegations they receive.

With a view to protecting human rights in the long term, it is important that peace settlements should provide for impartial investigations of past abuses. A process aimed at establishing the truth and measures to ensure that any perpetrators of human rights violations are brought to justice must be undertaken. Responsibility for human rights violations, past and present, must be made explicit, and general pre-conviction amnesties should not be part of peace settlements. Prior to peace negotiations, this would be an important part of any human rights education programmes you are able to organize.

If an international tribunal or a truth, justice and reconciliation commission is set up as part of the peace settlement, it is important that there is a formal role for human rights monitors in this stage of the process.

A difficult choice for a human rights organisation, or individual monitors, might be whether to advocate a cease-fire and play a role in conflict resolution. It is worth thinking about how this will impact on your impartiality.

Determining when you are dealing with "armed conflict" as defined in international humanitarian law: It is particularly important to know which international standards to apply. See the Introduction section to this booklet and the extracts from international humanitarian law attached in the Annexe II.

How to research and raise issues about arms transfers:[28]

These transactions are usually kept secret. However, there are numerous NGOs who are specifically researching these issues. If you suspect that your country is receiving weapons from country X, it might be worth contacting an arms trade NGOs in that country or institutes which carry out this research. The Internet is probably the best place to obtain up to date information on this subject. Here are some useful addresses:

UK:

World Development Movement
25 Beehive Place
London SW9 7QR
Tel: +41 20 7737 6215
Fax: +41 20 7274 8232
E-mail: wdm@wdm.org.uk
Web site: http://www.wdm.org.uk

Saferworld
3rd Floor, 34 Alfred Place
London WC1E 7DP
Tel: +41 20 7580 8866
Fax: +41 20 7631 1444
Email: sworld@gn.apc.org

28
A handbook on moitoring and documneting transfers and the use of small arms and torture equipment will be published in 2002

Mines Advisory Group
54A Main Street
Cockermouth
Cumbria CA13 9LU
Tel: +44 0900 828 580
Fax: +44 0900 827 088

Omega Foundation
6 Mount Street
Manchester M2 NS
Tel/fax: +44 161 831 9313
Email: omega@MCR1.poptel.org.uk

Iansa – International Action Network on Small Arms
Box 422
London WC1E 7BS
Email: contact@iansa.org
Web site: www.iansa.org

US:

Federation of American Scientists Arms Sales Monitoring Project
307 Massachusetts Avenue NE
Washington DC 2002
Tel: +1 202 675 1018
Web site: www.fas.org/asmp/library/handbook/cover.html

Council for a Livable World Education Fund
Thomas A Cardamone
110 Maryland Avenue NE
Suite 201
Washington DC 2001
E-mail: clw@clw.org
Web site: www.clw.org/cat/foraid/faidtoc.html

Human Rights Watch – Arms Division
350 Fifth Avenue
34th Floor
New York
NY 10018-3299
USA

E-mail: hrwnyc@hrw.org   Website: www.hrw.org

FRANCE:

Handicap International
ERAC
14 avenue Berthelot
69361 Lyon Cedex 07
Tel: +33 78 69 79 79
Fax: +33 78 69 79 94

Other Websites:
Coalition to Oppose the Arms Trade
Web site: www.ncf.carleton.ca/ip/global/coat

Arms Trade Database
Atdb.cdi.org

Annexes: International and regional standards

Annexe I: Relevant International human rights law – Full texts are available on the Internet

1. The International Covenant on Civil and Political Rights

Article 4 (1):
Allows for the derogation from certain rights "in time of public emergency which threatens the life of the nation and the existence of which is officially proclaimed...". However, Article 4(2) specifies that no derogation from "articles 6, 7, 8 (paragraphs 1 and 2), 11, 15, 16 and 18 may be made under this provision". Of particular relevance here are:

Article 6 (3):
When deprivation of life constitutes the crime of genocide, it is understood that nothing in this article shall authorize any State Party to the present Covenant to derogate in any way from any obligation assumed under the provisions of the Convention on the Prevention and Punishment of the Crime of Genocide.

Article 8 (1):
No one shall be held in slavery; slavery and the slave-trade in all their forms shall be prohibited.

Article 8 (2):
No one shall be held in servitude.

Article 20
1. Any propaganda for war shall be prohibited by law.
2. Any advocacy of national, racial or religious hatred that constitutes incitement to discrimination, hostility or violence shall be prohibited by law.

2. Convention against Torture and Other Cruel, Inhuman or Degrading Treatment or Punishment

Article 3:
No state may permit or tolerate torture or other cruel, inhuman or degrading treatment or punishment. Exceptional

circumstances such as a state of war or a threat of war, internal political instability or any other public emergency may not be invoked as a justification of torture or other cruel, inhuman or degrading treatment or punishment.

3. 1951 UN Convention relating to the Status of Refugees

4. UN Convention on the Elimination of Discrimination against Women

5. UN Declaration on the Protection of Women and Children in Emergency and Armed Conflicts

6. International Convention on the Elimination of All Forms of Racial Discrimination

Article 4

States Parties condemn all propaganda and all organizations which are based on ideas or theories of superiority of one race or group of persons of one colour or ethnic origin, or which attempt to justify or promote racial hatred and discrimination in any form, and undertake to adopt immediate and positive measures designed to eradicate all incitement to, or acts of, such discrimination and, to this end, with due regard to the principles embodied in the Universal Declaration of Human Rights and the rights expressly set forth in article 5 of this Convention, inter alia:

(a) Shall declare an offence punishable by law all dissemination of ideas based on racial superiority or hatred, incitement to racial discrimination, as well as all acts of violence or incitement to such acts against any race or group of persons of another colour or ethnic origin, and also the provision of any assistance to racist activities, including the financing thereof;

(b) Shall declare illegal and prohibit organizations, and also organized and all other propaganda activities, which promote and incite racial discrimination, and shall recognize participation in such organizations or activities as an offence punishable by law;

(c) Shall not permit public authorities or public institutions, national or local, to promote or incite racial discrimination.

7. UN Convention on the Prevention and Punishment of the Crime of Genocide

Article 1
The Contracting Parties confirm that genocide, whether committed in time of peace or in time of war, is a crime under international law which they undertake to prevent and to punish.

Article 2
In the present Convention, genocide means any of the following acts committed with intent to destroy, in whole or in part, a national, ethnical, racial or religious group, as such:
(a) Killing members of the group;
(b) Causing serious bodily or mental harm to members of the group;
(c) Deliberately inflicting on the group conditions of life calculated to bring about its physical destruction in whole or in part;
(d) Imposing measures intended to prevent births within the group;
(e) Forcibly transferring children of the group to another group.

Article 3
The following acts shall be punishable:
(a) Genocide;
(b) Conspiracy to commit genocide;
(c) Direct and public incitement to commit genocide;
(d) Attempt to commit genocide;
(e) Complicity in genocide.

Article 4
Persons committing genocide or any of the other acts enumerated in article III shall be punished, whether they are constitutionally responsible rulers, public officials or private individuals.

Article 6
Persons charged with genocide or any of the other acts enumerated in article III shall be tried by a competent tribunal of the State in the territory of which the act was

committed, or by such international penal tribunal as may have jurisdiction with respect to those Contracting Parties which shall have accepted its jurisdiction.

Article 7

Genocide and the other acts enumerated in article III shall not be considered as political crimes for the purpose of extradition.

The Contracting Parties pledge themselves in such cases to grant extradition in accordance with their laws and treaties in force.

8. UN Convention on the Rights of the Child

Article 38

1. State Parties undertake to respect and to ensure respect for rules of international humanitarian law applicable to them in armed conflicts which are relevant to the child.
2. State Parties shall take all feasible measures to ensure that persons who have not attained the age of fifteen years do not take a direct part in hostilities.
3. State Parties shall refrain from recruiting any person who has not attained the age of fifteen years into their armed forces. In recruiting among those persons who have attained the age of fifteen years but who have attained the age of eighteen years, State Parties shall endeavour to give priority to those who are oldest.
4. In accordance with their obligations under international humanitarian law to protect the civilian population in armed conflicts, State Parties shall take all feasible measures to ensure protection and care of children who are affected by an armed conflict.

Article 39

State Parties shall take all appropriate measures to promote physical and psychological recovery and social reintegration of a child victim of: any form of neglect, exploitation, or abuse; torture or any other form of cruel, inhuman or degrading treatment or punishment, or armed conflicts. Such recovery and reintegration shall take place in an environment which fosters the health, self-respect and dignity of the child.

Annexe II: International humanitarian law

1. Geneva Conventions and Additional Protocols (extracts):

Common Article 3 of the Geneva Conventions of August 12 1949:

In the case of armed conflict not of an international character occurring in the territory of one of the High Contracting Parties, each Party to the conflict shall be bound to apply, as a minimum, the following provisions:

(1) Persons taking no active part in the hostilities, including members of the armed forced who have laid down their arms and those placed *hors de combat* by sickness, wounds, detention, or any other cause, shall in all circumstances be treated humanely, without any adverse distinction founded on race, colour, religion or faith, sex, birth or wealth, or any other similar criteria.

To this end, the following acts are and shall remain prohibited at any time in any place whatsoever with respect to the above-mentioned persons:

(a) violence to life and person, in particular murder of all kinds, mutilation, cruel treatment and torture;

(b) taking of hostages;

(c) outrages upon personal dignity, in particular humiliating and degrading treatment;

(d) the passing of sentences and the carrying out of executions without previous judgement pronounced by a regularly constituted court, affording all the judicial guarantees which are recognized as indispensable by civilized peoples.

(2) The wounded and sick shall be collected and cared for.

An impartial humanitarian body, such as the International Committee of the Red Cross, may offer its services to the Parties to the conflict.

The Parties to the conflict should further endeavour to bring into force, by means of special agreements, all or part of the other provisions of the present Convention.

The application of the preceding provisions shall not affect the legal status of the Parties to the conflict.

Convention (IV) relative to the Protection of Civilian Persons in Time of War. Geneva, 12 August 1949

Article 34
The taking of hostages is prohibited.

Protocol Additional to the Geneva Conventions of 12 August 1949, and relating to the Protection of Victims of International Armed Conflicts (Protocol 1)

Section II—Combatant and Prisoner-of-War Status
Article 43 : Armed forces
1. The armed forces of a Party to a conflict consist of all organized armed forces, groups and units which are under a command responsible to that Party for the conduct of its subordinates, even if that Party is represented by a government or an authority not recognized by an adverse Party. Such armed forces shall be subject to an internal disciplinary system which, inter alia, shall enforce compliance with the rules of international law applicable in armed conflict.
2. Members of the armed forces of a Party to a conflict (other than medical personnel and chaplains covered by Article 33 of the Third Convention) are combatants, that is to say, they have the right to participate directly in hostilities.
3. Whenever a Party to a conflict incorporates a paramilitary or armed law enforcement agency into its armed forces it shall so notify the other Parties to the conflict.

Article 44: Combatants and prisoners of war
1. Any combatant, as defined in Article 43, who falls into the power of an adverse Party shall be a prisoner of war.

2. While all combatants are obliged to comply with the rules of international law applicable in armed conflict, violations of these rules shall not deprive a combatant of his right to be a combatant or, if he falls into the power

of an adverse Party, of his right to be a prisoner of war, except as provided in paragraphs 3 and 4.

3. In order to promote the protection of the civilian population from the effects of hostilities, combatants are obliged to distinguish themselves from the civilian population while they are engaged in an attack or in a military operation preparatory to an attack. Recognizing, however, that there are situations in armed conflicts where, owing to the nature of the hostilities an armed combatant cannot so distinguish himself, he shall retain his status as a combatant, provided that, in such situations, he carries his arms openly:

(a) During each military engagement, and

(b) During such time as he is visible to the adversary while he is engaged in a military deployment preceding the launching of an attack in which he is to participate.

Acts which comply with the requirements of this paragraph shall not be considered as perfidious within the meaning of Article 37, paragraph 1 (c).

4. A combatant who falls into the power of an adverse Party while failing to meet the requirements set forth in the second sentence of paragraph 3 shall forfeit his right to be a prisoner of war, but he shall, nevertheless, be given protections equivalent in all respects to those accorded to prisoners of war by the Third Convention and by this Protocol. This protection includes protections equivalent to those accorded to prisoners of war by the Third Convention in the case where such a person is tried and punished for any offences he has committed.

5. Any combatant who falls into the power of an adverse Party while not engaged in an attack or in a military operation preparatory to an attack shall not forfeit his rights to be a combatant and a prisoner of war by virtue of his prior activities.

6. This Article is without prejudice to the right of any person to be a prisoner of war pursuant to Article 4 of the Third Convention.

7. This Article is not intended to change the generally accepted practice of States with respect to the wearing of the uniform by combatants assigned to the regular, uniformed armed units of a Party to the conflict.

8. In addition to the categories of persons mentioned in Article 13 of the First and Second Conventions, all members of the armed forces of a Party to the conflict, as defined in Article 43 of this Protocol, shall be entitled to protection under those Conventions if they are wounded or sick or, in the case of the Second Convention, shipwrecked at sea or in other waters.

Article 45: Protection of persons who have taken part in hostilities

1. A person who takes part in hostilities and falls into the power of an adverse Party shall be presumed to be a prisoner of war, and therefore shall be protected by the Third Convention, if he claims the status of prisoner of war, or if he appears to be entitled to such status, or if the Party on which he depends claims such status on his behalf by notification to the detaining Power or to the Protecting Power. Should any doubt arise as to whether any such person is entitled to the status of prisoner of war, he shall continue to have such status and, therefore, to be protected by the Third Convention and this Protocol until such time as his status has been determined by a competent tribunal.

2. If a person who has fallen into the power of an adverse Party is not held as a prisoner of war and is to be tried by that Party for an offence arising out of the hostilities, he shall have the right to assert his entitlement to prisoner-of-war status before a judicial tribunal and to have that question adjudicated. Whenever possible under the applicable procedure, this adjudication shall occur before the trial for the offence. The representatives of the Protecting Power shall be entitled to attend the proceedings in which that question is adjudicated, unless, exceptionally, the proceedings are held in camera in the

interest of State security. In such a case the detaining Power shall advise the Protecting Power accordingly.

3. Any person who has taken part in hostilities, who is not entitled to prisoner-of-war status and who does not benefit from more favourable treatment in accordance with the Fourth Convention shall have the right at all times to the protection of Article 75 of this Protocol. In occupied territory, an such person, unless he is held as a spy, shall also be entitled, notwithstanding Article 5 of the Fourth Convention, to his rights of communication under that Convention.

Article 46: Spies

1. Notwithstanding any other provision of the Conventions or of this Protocol, any member of the armed forces of a Party to the conflict who falls into the power of an adverse Party while engaging in espionage shall not have the right to the status of prisoner of war and may be treated as a spy.

2. A member of the armed forces of a Party to the conflict who, on behalf of that Party and in territory controlled by an adverse Party, gathers or attempts to gather information shall not be considered as engaging in espionage if, while so acting, he is in the uniform of his armed forces.

3. A member of the armed forces of a Party to the conflict who is a resident of territory occupied by an adverse Party and who, on behalf of the Party on which he depends, gathers or attempts to gather information of military value within that territory shall not be considered as engaging in espionage unless he does so through an act of false pretences or deliberately in a clandestine manner. Moreover, such a resident shall not lose his right to the status of prisoner of war and may not be treated as a spy unless he is captured while engaging in espionage.

4. A member of the armed forces of a Patty to the conflict who is not a resident of territory occupied by an adverse

Party and who has engaged in espionage in that territory shall not lose his right to the status of prisoner of war and may not be treated as a spy unless he is captured before he has rejoined the armed forces to which he belongs.

Article 47: Mercenaries

1. A mercenary shall not have the right to be a combatant or a prisoner of war.

2. A mercenary is any person who:
(a) Is specially recruited locally or abroad in order to fight in an armed conflict;
(b) Does, in fact, take a direct part in the hostilities;
(c) Is motivated to take part in the hostilities essentially by the desire for private gain and, in fact, is promised, by or on behalf of a Party to the conflict, material compensation substantially in excess of that promised or paid to combatants of similar ranks and functions in the armed forces of that Party;
(d) Is neither a national of a Party to the conflict nor a resident of territory controlled by a Party to the conflict;
(e) Is not a member of the armed forces of a Party to the conflict; and
(f) Has not been sent by a State which is not a Party to the conflict on official duty as a member of its armed forces.

PART IV: CIVILIAN POPULATION

Section I: General Protection Against Effects of Hostilities

Chapter 1: Basic Rule and Field of Application

Article 48: Basic rule
In order to ensure respect for and protection of the civilian population and civilian objects, the Parties to the conflict shall at all times distinguish between the civilian population and

combatants and between civilian objects and military objectives and accordingly shall direct their operations only against military objectives.

Article 49: Definition of attacks and scope of application

1. "Attacks" means acts of violence against the adversary, whether in offence or in defence.
2. The provisions of this Protocol with respect to attacks apply to all attacks in whatever territory conducted, including the national territory belonging to a Party to the conflict but under the control of an adverse Party.

3. The provisions of this Section apply to any land, air or sea warfare which may affect the civilian population, individual civilians or civilian objects on land. They further apply to all attacks from the sea or from the air against objectives on land but do not otherwise affect the rules of international law applicable in armed conflict at sea or in the air.

4. The provisions of this Section are additional to the rules concerning humanitarian protection contained in the Fourth Convention, particularly in Part II thereof, and in other international agreements binding upon the High Contracting Parties, as well as to other rules of international law relating to the protection of civilians and civilian objects on land, at sea or in the air against the effects of hostilities.

Chapter II: Civilians and Civil Population

Article 50: Definition of civilians and civilian population

1. A civilian is any person who does not belong to one of the categories of persons referred to in Article 4 A (1), (2), (3) and (6) of the Third Convention and in Article 43 of this Protocol. In case of doubt whether a person is a civilian, that person shall be considered to be a civilian.
2. The civilian population comprises all persons who are civilians.

3. The presence within the civilian population of individuals who do not come within the definition of civilians does not deprive the population of its civilian character.

Article 51: Protection of the civilian population

1. The civilian population and individual civilians shall enjoy general protection against dangers arising from military operations. To give effect to this protection, the following rules, which are additional to other applicable rules of international law, shall be observed in circumstances.

2. The civilian population as such, as well as individual civilians, shall not be the object of attack. Acts or threats of violence the primary purpose of which is to spread terror among the civilian population are prohibited.

3. Civilians shall enjoy the protection afforded by this Section, unless and for such time as they take a direct part in hostilities.

4. Indiscriminate attacks are prohibited. Indiscriminate attacks are:
(a) Those which are not directed at a specific military objective;
(b) Those which employ a method or means of combat which cannot be directed at a specific military objective; or
(c) Those which employ a method or means of combat the effects of which cannot be limited as required by this Protocol; and consequently, in each such case, are of a nature to strike military objectives and civilians or civilian objects without distinction.

5. Among others, the following types of attacks are to be considered as indiscriminate:
(a) An attack by bombardment by any methods or means which treats as a single military objective a number of clearly separated and distinct military

objectives located in a city, town, village or other area containing a similar concentration of civilians or civilian objects; and

(b) An attack which may be expected to cause incidental loss of civilian life, injury to civilians, damage to civilian objects, or a combination thereof, which would be excessive in relation to the concrete and direct military advantage anticipated.

6. Attacks against the civilian population or civilians by way of reprisals are prohibited.

7. The presence or movements of the civilian population or individual civilians shall not be used to render certain points or areas immune from military operations, in particular in attempts to shield military objectives from attacks or to shield, favour or impede military operations. The Parties to the conflict shall not direct the movement of the civilian population or individual civilians in order to attempt to shield military objectives from attacks or to shield military operations.

8. Any violation of these prohibitions shall not release the Parties to the conflict from their legal obligations with respect to the civilian population and civilians, including the obligation to take the precautionary measures provided for in Article 57.

Chapter III—Civilian Objects

Article 52: General protection of civilian objects

1. Civilian objects shall not be the object of attack or of reprisals. Civilian objects are all objects which are not military objectives as defined in paragraph 2.

2. Attacks shall be limited strictly to military objectives. In so far as objects are concerned, military objectives are limited to those objects which by their nature, location, purpose or use make an effective contribution to military action and whose total or partial destruction, capture or neutralization, in the

circumstances ruling at the time, offers a definite military of advantage.

In case of doubt whether an object which is normally dedicated to civilian purposes, such as a place of worship, a house or other dwelling or a school, is being used to make an effective contribution to military action, it shall be presumed not to be so used.

Article 53: Protection of cultural objects and of places of worship

Without prejudice to the provisions of the Hague Convention for the Protection of Cultural Property in the Event of Armed Conflict of 14 May 1954, and of other relevant international instruments, it is prohibited:

(a) To commit any acts of hostility directed against the historic monuments, works of art or places of worship which constitute the cultural or spiritual heritage of peoples;

(b) To use such objects in support of the military effort;

(c) To make such objects the object of reprisals.

Article 54: Protection of objects indispensable to the survival of the civilian population

1. Starvation of civilians as a method of warfare is prohibited.

2. It is prohibited to attack, destroy, remove or render useless objects indispensable to the survival of the civilian population, such as foodstuffs, agricultural areas for the production of foodstuffs, crops, livestock, drinking water installations and supplies and irrigation works, for the specific purpose of denying them for their sustenance value to the civilian population or to the adverse Party, whatever the motive, whether in order to starve out civilians, to cause them to move away, or for any other motive.

3. The prohibitions in paragraph 2 shall not apply to such of the objects covered by it as are used by an adverse Party:

(a) As sustenance solely for the members of its armed forces; or

(b) If not as sustenance, then in direct support of military action, provided, however, that in no event shall actions against these objects be taken which may be expected to leave the civilian population with such inadequate food or water as to cause its starvation or force its movement.

4. These objects shall not be made the object of reprisals.

5. In recognition of the vital requirements of any Party to the conflict in the defence of its national territory against invasion, derogation from the prohibitions contained in paragraph 2 may be made by a Party to the conflict within such territory under its own control where required by imperative military necessity.

Chapter IV—Precautionary Measures

Article 57: Precautions in attack

1. In the conduct of military operations, constant care shall be taken to spare the civilian population, civilians and civilian objects.

2. With respect to attacks, the following precautions shall be taken:

(a) Those who plan or decide upon an attack shall:

(i) Do everything feasible to verify that the objectives to be attacked are neither civilians nor civilian objects and are not subject to special protection but are military objectives within the meaning of paragraph 2 of Article 52 and that it is not prohibited by the provisions of this Protocol to attack them;

(ii) Take all feasible precautions in the choice of means and methods of attack with a view to avoiding, and in any event to minimizing, incidental loss of civilian life, injury to civilians and damage to civilian objects;

(iii) Refrain from deciding to launch any attack which may be expected to cause incidental loss of civilian life, injury to civilians, damage to civilian objects, or a combination thereof, which would be excessive in relation to the concrete and direct military advantage anticipated;

(b) An attack shall be cancelled or suspended if it becomes apparent that the objective is not a military one or is subject to special protection or that the attack may be expected to cause incidental loss of civilian life, injury to civilians, damage to civilian objects, or a combination thereof, which would be excessive in relation to the concrete and direct military advantage anticipated;

(c) Effective advance warning shall be given of attacks which may affect the civilian population, unless circumstances do not permit.

3. When a choice is possible between several military objectives for obtaining a similar military advantage, the objective to be selected shall be that the attack on which may be expected to cause the least danger to civilian lives and to civilian objects.

4. In the conduct of military operations at sea or in the air, each Party to the conflict shall, in conformity with its rights and duties under the rules of international law applicable in armed conflict, take all reasonable precautions to avoid losses of civilian lives and damage to civilian objects.

5. No provision of this Article may be construed as authorizing any attacks against the civilian population, civilians or civilian objects.

Article 58: Precautions against the effects of attacks

The Parties to the conflict shall, to the maximum extent feasible:

(a) Without prejudice to Article 49 of the Fourth Convention, endeavour to remove the civilian population, individual civilians and civilian objects under their control from the vicinity of military objectives;

(b) Avoid locating military objectives within or near densely populated areas;

(c) Take the other necessary precautions to protect the civilian population, individual civilians and civilian objects under their control against the dangers resulting from military operations.

Article 77(2)

The Parties to the conflict shall take all feasible measures in order that children who have not attained the age of fifteen years do not take a direct part in hostilities and, in particular, they shall refrain from recruiting them into their armed forces. In recruiting among these persons who have attained the age of fifteen years but who have not attained the age of eighteen years, the Parties to the conflict shall endeavour to give priority to those who are oldest."

1977 Protocol Additional to the Geneva Conventions of 12 August 1949, and Relating to the Protection of Victims of Non-International Armed Conflicts (Protocol II)

Part II—Humane Treatment

Article 4: Fundamental guarantees

1. All persons who do not take a direct part or who have ceased to take part in hostilities, whether or not their liberty has been restricted, are entitled to respect for their person, honour and convictions and religious practices. They shall in all circumstances be treated humanely, without any adverse distinction. It is prohibited to order that there shall be no survivors.

2. Without prejudice to the generality of the foregoing, the following acts against the persons referred to in paragraph 1 are and shall remain prohibited at any time and in any place whatsoever:

(a) violence to the life, health and physical or mental well-being of persons, in particular murder as well as cruel treatment such as torture mutilation or any form of corporal punishment;

(b) collective punishments;

(c) taking of hostages;

(d) acts of terrorism;

(e) outrages upon personal dignity, in particular humiliating and degrading treatment, rape enforced prostitution and any form of indecent assault;

(f) slavery and the slave trade in all their forms;

(g) pillage;

(h) threats to commit any of the foregoing acts.

3. Children shall be provided with the care and aid they require, and in particular:

(a) they shall receive an education, including religious and moral education, in keeping with the wishes of their parents, or in the absence of their parents, of those responsible for their care;

(b) all appropriate steps shall be taken to facilitate the reunion of families temporarily separated;

(c) children who have not attained the age of fifteen years shall neither be recruited in the armed forces or groups nor allowed to take part in hostilities;

(d) the special protection provided by this Article to children who have not attained the age of fifteen years shall remain applicable to them if they take a direct part of hostilities despite the provisions of sub-paragraph (c) and are captured;

(e) measures shall be taken, if necessary, and whenever possible with the consent of their parents or persons who by law or custom are primarily responsible for their care, to remove children temporarily from the area in which hostilities are taking place to a safer area within the country and ensure that they are accompanied by persons responsible for their safety and well-being.

Article 5: Persons whose liberty has been restricted

1. In addition to the provisions of Article 4, the following provisions shall be respected as a minimum with regard to persons deprives of their liberty for reasons related to the armed conflict, whether they are interned or detained:

(a) the wounded and the sick shall be treated in accordance with Article 7;

(b) the persons referred to in this paragraph shall, to the same extent as the local civilian population, be provided with food and drinking water and be afforded safeguards as regards health and hygiene and protection against the rigours of the climate and the dangers of the armed conflict.

(c) they shall be allowed to receive individual or collective relief;

(d) they shall be allowed to practise their religion and, if requested and appropriate, to receive spiritual assistance from persons, such as chaplains, performing religious functions;

(e) they shall, if made to work, have the benefit of working conditions and safeguards similar to those enjoyed by the local civilian population.

2. Those who are responsible for the internment or detention of the persons referred to in paragraph 1 shall also, within the limits of their capabilities, respect the following provisions relating to such persons:

(a) except when men and women of a family are accommodated together, women shall be held in quarters separated from those of men and shall be under the immediate supervision of women;

(b) they shall be allowed to send and receive letters and cards, the number of which may be limited by competent authority as it deems necessary;

(c) places of internment and detention shall not be located close to the combat zone. The persons referred to in paragraph 1 shall be evacuated when the places where they are interned or detained become particularly exposed to danger arising out of the armed conflict, if their evacuation can be carried out under adequate conditions of safety;

(d) they shall have the benefit of medical examinations;

(e) their physical or mental health and integrity shall not be endangered by an unjustified act or omissions. Accordingly, it is prohibited to subject the persons described in this Article to any medical procedure which is not indicated by the state of health of the person concerned, and which is not consistent with the generally accepted medical standards applied to free persons under similar medical circumstances.

3. Persons who are not covered by paragraph 1 but whose liberty ha been restricted in any way whatsoever for reasons related to the armed conflict shall be treated humanely in accordance with Article 4 and with paragraphs 1 (a), (c) and (d), and 2 (b) of this Article.

4. If it is decided to release persons deprived of their liberty, necessary measures to ensure their safety shall be taken by those so deciding.

Article 6: Penal prosecutions

1. This Article applies to the prosecution and punishment of criminal offences related to the armed conflict.

2. No sentence shall be passed and no penalty shall be executed on a person found guilty of an offence except pursuant to a conviction pronounced by a court offering the essential guarantees of independent and impartiality. In particular:

(a) the procedure shall provide for an accused to be informed without delay of the particulars of the offence alleged against him and shall afford the accused before and during his trial all necessary rights and means of defence;

(b) no one shall be convicted of an offence except on the basis of individual penal responsibility;

(c) no one shall be convicted of an offence on account of any act or omission which did not constitute a criminal offence, under the law, at the time when it was committed; nor shall a heavier penalty be imposed that that which was applicable at the time when the criminal offence was committed; if, after the commission of the offence, provision is made by law for the imposition of a lighter penalty, the offender shall benefit thereby;

(d) anyone charged with an offence is presumed

innocent until proved guilty according to law;

(e) anyone charged with an offence shall have the right to be tried in his presence;

(f) no one shall be compelled to testify against himself or to confess guilt

3.A convicted person shall be advised on conviction of his judicial and other remedies and of the time-limited within which they may be exercised.

4.The death penalty shall not be pronounced on persons who were under the age of eighteen years at the time of the offence and shall not be carried out on pregnant women or mothers of young children.

5.At the end of hostilities, the authorities in power shall endeavour to grant the broadest possible amnesty to persons who have participated in the armed conflict, or those deprived of their liberty for reasons related to the armed conflict, whether they are interned or detained.

Part IV—Civilian Population

Article 13: Protection of the civilian population

1.The civilian population and individual civilians shall enjoy general protection against the dangers arising from military operations. To give effect to this protection, the following rules shall be observed in all circumstances.

2.The civilian population as such, as well as individual civilians, shall not be the object of attack. Acts or threats of violence the primary purpose of which is to spread terror among the civilian population are prohibited.

3.Civilians shall enjoy the protection afforded by this Part, unless and for such time as they take a direct part in hostilities.

Article 14: Protection of objects indispensable to the survival of the civilian population

Starvation of civilians as a method of combat is prohibited. It is therefore prohibited to attack, destroy, remove or render useless, for that purpose, objects indispensable to the survival of the civilian population, such as foodstuffs, agricultural areas for the production of foodstuffs, crops, livestock, drinking water installations and supplies and irrigation works.

Article 17: Prohibition of forced movement of civilians

1. The displacement of the civilian population shall not be ordered for reasons related to the conflict unless the security of the civilians involved or imperative military reasons so demand. Should such displacements have to be carried out, all possible measure shall be taken in order that the civilian population may be received under satisfactory conditions of shelter, hygiene, health, safety and nutrition.

2. Civilians shall not be compelled to leave their own territory for reasons connected with the conflict.

Annex III: Regional Human Rights Standards

1974 Organization of African Unity (OAU) Convention governing the specific aspects of refugee problems in Africa:

Article 1

Definition of the term "Refugee"

1. For the purposes of this Convention, the term "refugee" shall mean every person who, owing to well-founded fear of being persecuted for reasons of race, religion, nationality, membership of a particular social group or political opinion, is outside the country of his nationality and is unable or, owing to such fear, is unwilling to avail himself of the protection of that country, or who, not having a nationality and being outside the country of his former habitual residence as a result of such events is unable or, owing to such fear, is unwilling to return to it.

2. The term "refugee" shall also apply to every person who, owing to external aggression, occupation, foreign domination or events seriously disturbing public order in either part or the whole of his country of origin or nationality, is compelled to leave his place of habitual residence in order to seek refuge in another place outside his country of origin or nationality.

3. In the case of a person who has several nationalities, the term "a country of which he is a national" shall mean each of the countries of which he is a national, and a person shall not be deemed to be lacking the protection of the country of which he is a national if, without any valid reason based on well-founded fear, he has not availed himself of the protection of one of the countries of which he is a national.

Article 2

3. No person shall be subjected by a Member State to measures such as rejection at the frontier, return or expulsion, which would compel him to return to or remain in a territory where his life, physical integrity or liberty would be threatened for the reasons set out in Article I, paragraphs 1 and 2.

4. Where a Member State finds difficulty in continuing to grant asylum to refugees, such Member State may appeal directly to other Member States and through the OAU, and such other Member States shall in the spirit of African solidarity and international co-operation take appropriate measures to lighten the burden of the Member State granting asylum.

5. Where a refugee has not received the right to reside in any country of asylum, he may be granted temporary residence in any country of asylum in which he first presented himself as a refugee pending arrangement for his resettlement in accordance with the preceding paragraph.

6. For reasons of security, countries of asylum shall, as far as possible, settle refugees at a reasonable distance from the frontier of their country of origin.

Article 5

Voluntary Repatriation

1. The essentially voluntary character of repatriation shall be respected in all cases and no refugee shall be repatriated against his will.

2. The country of asylum, in collaboration with the country of origin, shall make adequate arrangements for the safe return of refugees who request repatriation.

3. The country of origin, on receiving back refugees, shall facilitate their resettlement and grant them the full rights and privileges of nationals of the country, and subject them to the same obligations.

4. Refugees who voluntarily return to their country shall in no way be penalized for having left it for any of the reasons giving rise to refugee situations. Whenever necessary, an appeal shall be made through national information media and through the Administrative Secretary-General of the OAU, inviting refugees to return home and giving assurance that the new circumstances prevailing in their country of origin will enable them to return without risk and to take up a normal and peaceful life without fear of being disturbed or punished, and that the text of such appeal should be given to refugees and clearly explained to them by their country of asylum.

5. Refugees who freely decide to return to their homeland, as a result of such assurances or on their own initiative, shall be given every possible assistance by the country of asylum, the country of origin, voluntary agencies and international and intergovernmental organizations, to facilitate their return.

OAU African Charter on Human and Peoples' Rights

Article 5:
Every individual shall have the right to respect for the dignity inherent in a human being and to the recognition of his legal status. All forms of exploitation and degradation of man, particularly slavery, slave trade, torture, cruel, inhuman or degrading punishment and treatment shall be prohibited.

OAU Convention for the Elimination of Mercenaries in Africa of July 3 1977, came into effect in 1985.

For full details see Internet www.oau-oau.org

The Publishers

Amnesty International (AI) is a worldwide voluntary activist movement working towards the observance of all human rights as enshrined in the Universal Declaration of Human Rights and other international standards. It promotes respect for human rights, which it considers interdependent and indivisible, through campaigning and public awareness activities, as well as through human rights education and pushing for ratification and implementation of human rights treaties. Amnesty International takes action against violations by governments of people's civil and political rights. It is independent of any government, political persuasion or religious creed. It does not support or oppose any government or political system, nor does it support or oppose the views of the victims whose rights it seeks to protect. It is concerned solely with the impartial protection of human rights.

Amnesty International Dutch Section Special Programme on Africa (SPA) was established in 1994. Initially, SPA developed a programme to assist Amnesty Sections worldwide to improve the effectiveness of their campaigning against human rights violations in Africa. Since 1996 SPA has moved towards providing support to the broader Human Rights Movement in Africa. Rather than funding projects, SPA is developing and co-ordinating long term projects for and and in cooperation with other human rights organisations and AI sections. In addition to copublishing *Ukweli*, SPA is also coordinating advocacy and training workshops in southern and West Africa, a project on policing and Human Rights, and a pilot project to raise human rights awareness in rural areas in Liberia.

CODESRIA is the Council for the Development of Social Science Research in Africa head-quartered in Dakar, Senegal. It is an independent organisation whose principal objectives are facilitating research, promoting research-based publishing and creating multiple forums geared towards the exchange of views and information among African researchers. It challenges the fragmentation of research through the creation of thematic research networks that cut across linguistic and regional boundaries.

CODESRIA publishes a quarterly journal, *Africa Development*, the longest standing Africa-based social science journal; *Afrika Zamani*, a journal of history; the *African Sociological Review*, and the *African Journal of International Affairs (AJIA)*. Research results and other activities of the institution are disseminated through 'Working Papers', 'Monograph Series', 'New Path Series', 'State-of-the-Literature Series', 'CODESRIA Book Series', and the *CODESRIA Bulletin*.